# A History of RADFORD

## Compiled by Brian D. R. Steele

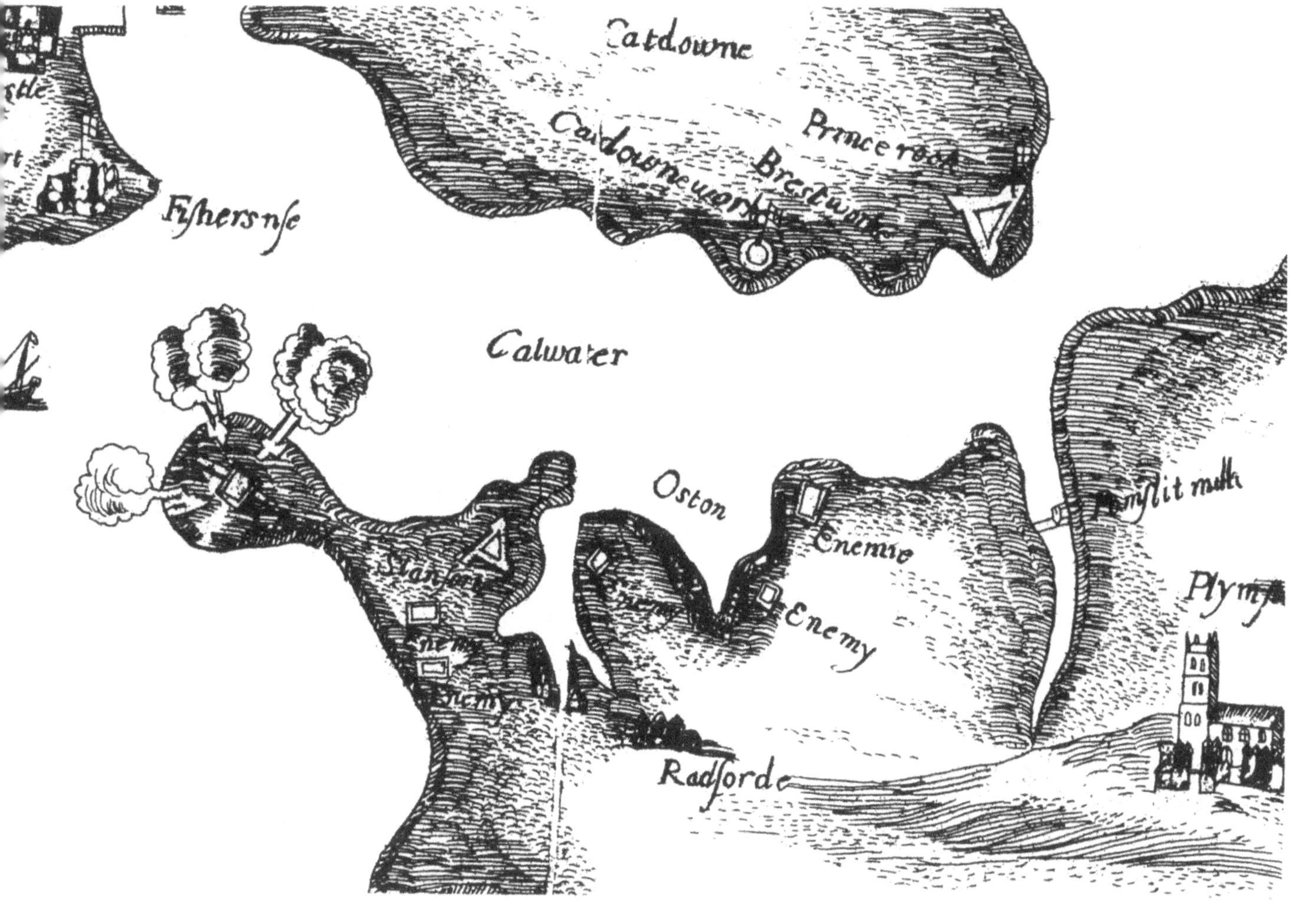

Fig. 20: Part of the siege map of Plymouth dated 1643 showing Radford.

This version of the book is virtually as originally published, presenting the work of Brian D. R. Steele. There are now additional pages at the back providing information about the publisher, Arthur L Clamp.

The republishing project is being managed by Arthur's grandson, Steven Gibson. We aim to find all the research that he was involved in publishing, preserving it for the next generation as part of 'The Clamp Collection'.

## INTRODUCTION

In 1978 my attention was drawn to a newspaper advertisement in the *Western Evening Herald*. Plymouth city council were inviting tenders to take on a lease for the Pond Farm at Radford dip. I was not familiar with the farm but I was interested in the idea of establishing an Adventure Centre in the area.

At that time I was managing the Morley Youth and Community Centre and consequently envisaged some type of annexe to Morley being developed. Based upon this whimsical idea, a group of leaders and members visited Pond Farm.

The building was a disaster of dilapidation. Much of the roof gone, timber rotted, walls cracked and crumbling — it still amazes me that we clambered over this ruin and talked excitedly about rebuilding the place. We departed making optimistic noises intent on contacting the City Council.

The next day we put in our bid for Pond Farm (apparently the only other bid was from a chicken farmer). In the course of time the city let us have it for a peppercorn rent on the basis that we renovate it within a fixed period. Well, it was ours, and we now visited the ruin with a little more caution. Being a collection of amateurs, we believed much of the restoration work could be undertaken by ourselves so we set about clearing debris (incidently several tons of cow dung had to be removed). We even secured all doors and windows, such was our concept of its value! To most people passing by at that time, Pond Farm was a ruin beyond repair; to us it was a challenge.

Over the next ten years a group of dedicated people worked hard raising money through raft races, fayres, car boot sales and other sources. The city lottery contributed greatly and other charities aided us until little by little the ruin was transformed into the *Radford Adventure and Field Study Centre*.

Support and money was given freely but our greatest asset was always the *free labour*. Projects like *Pathfinders* and *Community Programme* were agencies that enabled us to achieve our objective.

In 1987 the building was finished and Mr. Bill Mayers, the Project chairman, negotiated with D.C.C. Social Services to use the new building as a day Centre for Special Needs people. This usage, together with regular Youth Group lettings and visits from schools, has made Radford a valuable resource in the area. A place people can visit and find out more about the plant and animal life of the area and in particular the history of a valley that has been inhabited for over 1,000 years.

Many people have lived in this valley. Over the centuries hopes, fears, loves, hates, laughter and tears have all been felt by people who belonged to Radford. *Radford was home*.

The next few pages will touch a little on some of these conditions. It is not a definitive History of Radford, but just a touch and feel of the people and things that happened, a dip into time; a flavour of how it was then.

Brian D. R. Steele,
Founder Member Radford Centre,
February, 1990.

## ACKNOWLEDGEMENTS

I am greatly indebted to the following for their support and time without whose help this account of Radford would not have been possible. The Radford Centre, *for financing this publication*, Mrs. Vera Lambert, Hooe Road, Mr. Neill P. G. Mitchell, *who supplied considerable photographic and written material*, G. W. Copeland, Devonshire Association's *Report and Transactions 1945*, Rev. John Swete's Journal, Devon County Record Office, *information and photographs*, Mr. Terry Phillips, Hooe, Mr. Harold Twiggs, Looe, *builder contracted to demolish Radford in 1937*, Miss Audrey M. Wood, Higher Hooe, *information and postcards*, Mr. Gordon, builder who renovated Radford Lodge, Mr. Arthur L. Clamp, local historian, Western Morning News, *photographs*, S. A. Wightman Ltd, *photographs*, Mr. Christopher Harris Bulteel, and Mr. Richard Hillersden Bulteel, *information and photographs*, Mr. Fred Rowland, *information*, Mrs. Smout, *information on St. Keverns*, Mr. Steve Ash, *photographs and genealogical information*, Local History Library, *information and photographs*, Exeter Central Library, *William Payne painting 1793*, Mrs. Verena Reed, *typescript production*, and Mr. David Dane, *photographic support*.

# POND FARM RADFORD

The Radford Adventure and Field Study Centre now stands on the site once occupied by Pond Farm. This name refers to its position by the ornamental ponds and is of recent origin. Also known as *Duck Ponds* which is quite obvious whenever you go down to the lake!

This was a collection of old farm buildings built on the estate about 1750. Evidence of the age of the buildings was found when excavations of the long barn brought to light a foundation stone. This stone, with the inscription *W.M. W.H. 1780* can be seen in the Radford Centre. (The initials being those of the mason and his apprentice). It is likely that some parts of the building date back later than this. The evidence of this is found in a very detailed journal written by Rev. John Swete in 1793. He was born in 1752, and between 1792 and 1800 he made a series of tours of Devon. His journal contains a visit he made to Plymstock.

In it he relates his impressions and feelings at the time, coupled with watercolour sketches of remarkable clarity. A sample of his actual handwriting is shown here (Fig. 1) and his drawing of Radford Mill (Fig. 7) on Page 6.

*The assemblage of rurale traits of the most charming natures here met in the happiest disposition – the road. the mill the wood the foamy water fall*

Of course we cannot be sure where this mill stood because, to the best of our knowledge, there is no trace of it today. However, his description leads us to speculate that the location could only have been at Radford dip. The view he painted shows the mill somewhere between the road and the boathouse (which appears in the background). Also Radford Lake was referred to as *Mill Pond* in the tythe map of 1843. In an article by J. W. Perkins it is suggested that the mill was most probably worked by a leat built to run along the south side of Radford dip and that references made about secret passages and tunnels refers to this leat which would have embodied a tunnel running under the road.

The Rev. John Swete referred to this area as an *assemblage of rural traits of the most Charming Nature here meet in the happiest disposition ... the Mill ... the Wood ... the foaming Waterfall ... is a very uncommon circumstance to behold the tide visiting so rural a collection of objects.*

There can be no doubt that the mill was in Radford dip because his journal describes leaving the scene and *passed through the gate opposite, hoping for a view of Radford House.* He got this view but was very disappointed and made some derogatory comments about the building and its location. This was probably because he had high expectations of what a family mansion should look like. Also the fact that he continued up the hill to Hooe Manor and was very impressed with the house and grounds, (see Fig. 25 on Page 24). John Swete has made an exceptional contribution to what life was like at that time.

No other record of the mill or farm buildings exist until present times when the 1917 bankruptcy sale referred to the buildings as *conveniently arranged and well built cowsheds and other farm buildings in the occupation of Mr. Atwill.* In the 1940s several watercolour paintings by Robert Stitson show the long barn as being two storey, but at this time it was a dilapidated cowshed and remained so until 1978 when the Radford Project was started.

An engraved stone, which is thought to refer to Isaiah Harris, is laid into the wall of the long barn, but why it was produced and why placed in that wall is unknown. It is dated 1774 (Fig. 2).

In 1944 a Mr. Sydney Phillips was to occupy the farm and could be seen into the 1970s tending his cows and moving them from the milking sheds to the meadows. During the war sixteen of his cows and a horse were killed outside the farm building by anti-personnel bombs. Much later, in the 1950s, a single cow was to cause much consternation when she apparently fell down a hole close to the Radford House site. Initially people thought she had literally stumbled upon the Radford secret passage, but on winching her to safety, found she had merely fallen into a long disused water storage tank most of which had to be dug away to get her out!

## RADFORD AND THE HARRIS FAMILY

The early history of Radford is not very well documented. There have been various Roman and Bronze age references and undoubtedly, because of the location of Radford, it is likely that various settlements would have existed.

Easy access to the sea and good cultivation and grazing land would have been very attractive to early man. All structures in those times would have been made from timber, consequently no evidence has been found but we can surmise no doubt, like so many other instances, some unwitting landowner had his lands confiscated when the Normans arrived!

Our most reliable documentation appears in the *Survey of Devon* (1714) in which Tristan Risdon records that William le Abbé of Norman descent held the lands in the reign of Henry III (1216-1272).

The name Radford comes from *REDFORD* which is attributed to the colour of the soil (although it doesn't seem to be particularly red). Tristan Risdon also intimated that le Abbé's son Walter, also known as Walterus de Radford, was the first member of the family to assume the name Radford. Little is known of the Radfords except to say that Risdon noted thereafter ... *continued their dwelling in this place divers descendants.*

The next record that Risdon refers to is that of the eminent Harris family who managed Radford for more than four centuries and who were the family to make Radford great. It is probable that in the reign of Edward VI (1461-1483) the estate came into the hands of the Harris family but it may have been earlier. In the *Visitation of the Heralds* a John Harris was at Radford which dates the families residence at circa 1413. In Plymstock's parish church of St. Mary and All Saints, there are several memorials mounted in the Lady Chapel bearing witness to the Harris family influence (these relate to the 17th, 18th and 19th centuries).

In 1549 William Harris was sent to Fleet Prison in London for a short period for his part in the Great Western Rebellion when some men of Devon and Cornwall protested against the new prayer book introduced by Edward VI. William Harris's son Christopher was the next in line and at the tender age of five years inherited the estate.

The Radford Estate today, is to the casual observer another 1970s housing development, a pleasant area to live; located in a sweeping valley surmounted by trees. Some will say that the valley has retained much of its natural beauty despite the building development; others bewail this modern intrusion which has disfigured a once beautiful valley. Whatever viewpoint you take, we cannot change what has happened. We can only endeavour to preserve what remains for the future. If the residents of Radford over the centuries could return now they would undoubtedly be dumbfounded at the enormous changes that have occured in such a relatively short period of time. Conversely, if we could go back in time we also would be amazed at the important role Radford had in the past considering the lack of evidence today. As mentioned before, to the casual observer it is a modern estate, but delve back a little and Radford's outstanding historical importance is revealed.

Comparatively few people are aware of the prominent role Radford has played in Plymouth. Just over 50 years ago one of the most tangible reminders of the valley's illustrious past was demolished. 600 years of habitation disappeared when Radford House was raised to the ground in 1937. At the time of the demolition it was undoubtedly a rambling ruin but nevertheless, it was a fifty roomed mansion of monumental proportions. As can be seen from the various prints of the house (Figs. 3, 4, 5), it was an impressive residence and hence reflected the status and importance of the owners throughout the centuries.

The House was not unattractive, set in its low position at the head of Radford Lake and surrounded by parkland, lawns and picturesque gardens (Fig. 5). Because of the importance of Radford it was inevitable that the names of famous people be associated with it. There is no doubt that the flamboyant lifestyles of the great Elizabethans, Drake, Hawkins, Howard, Raleigh, etc., were to be seen at Radford on many occasions as was the excitement and tragedy of the Civil War and its aftermath (Fig. 8).

Fig. 3: Radford House in landscape from the sketch books of William Payne, Volume II, about 1793.

Fig. 4: A very rare photograph of the interior of Radford House showing the wood-panelled dining room, furniture and the table partly arranged for a meal. Taken in the early years of this century.

Fig. 5: Radford House seen in about 1928 a matter of a few years before its demolition. This postcard scene is still well remembered by many local people.

Christopher Harris (Fig. 9) was to be one of the most influential men of his day. He became a close personal friend of Francis Drake (1540-1596) and often carried out transactions on his behalf. In 1585, for example, when Drake wished to purchase Buckland Abbey, its owner, Sir Richard Grenville, disliked Drake so intensely that he would not sell. Consequently Christopher Harris purchased the Abbey in his own name and then transferred it to Drake six months later, the purchase price being £3,400. Drake's confidence in Harris is reflected by his decision, recorded in the *Western Antiquary* of 1886 (written by the former Plymouth Librarian, W. H. K. Wright), to store at Radford ... *some of the gold and silver in blocks which that daring seaman brought home with him from the South Seas.*

Inevitably it was at Drake's instigation that Christopher Harris stood for the new Parliament called by Elizabeth I in 1584. In view of Drake's personal interest in a scheme to bring fresh water to Plymouth it is hardly surprising that it fell to Harris to present the Water Bill in the House of Commons, which later came into effect in 1591.

The defeat of the Armada in 1588 (Fig. 10) was the cause for great celebration in Plymouth and Christopher Harris duly hosted at Radford the victory banquet in honour of Drake, Raleigh, Howard, Hawkings and the other Captains who had so successfully fought the Spanish Fleet. Drake eventually died at sea in 1596 and Harris acted as one of his executors.

Christopher Harris was knighted by James I on the 7th June, 1609, and died in 1625. Two monuments, erected circa 1635 and 1677 respectively on either side of the east window of the parish church's Lady Chapel, act as the only memorial to this remarkable man.

Fig. 6:

One of the very few stones recording part of the story of Radford mansion and the Harris family.

Fig. 7: Radford Mill watercolour sketch by Rev. John Swete, 1793.

This is the earliest known map of the Plymouth area showing Radford under the ownership of the Harris family. It dates from the 1500s and records what the area was like at the height of the great seafaring adventures of the Elizabethans.

Fig. 10: This dramatic scene depicts one of the sea battles which led to the defeat of the Spanish Armada in 1588. Many of these ships were based at Plymouth and came under the command of Sir Francis Drake. Queen Elizabeth I's fleet was then moored in the Cattewater to which the Harris's had quick and easy access.

# SIR WALTER RALEIGH (1552-1618)

Sir Walter Raleigh was a close friend of Christopher Harris. It is a sad irony that Harris held Raleigh under house arrest at Radford on his return in 1618 from the disastrous gold expedition to Guiana in Venezuela.

In June, 1618, Raleigh arrived back in Plymouth only to find that King James had an order out for his arrest. His abortive search for a gold mine and the death of his son Wat on this expedition had sapped his spirit and he willingly surrendered himself to the King's representative. During the next few weeks he was held at Radford in company with his wife Bess and his companion Captain Samuel King.

Sir Lewis Stukely, Vice Admiral of Devon, was responsible for Raleigh during this period but he appeared to pay little attention to his charge, allowing Raleigh plenty of freedom whilst he rode about the countryside.

In Captain King's diary of the period he mentions that Raleigh did eventually consider escape and asked King to arrange a barque to convey him to France.

This Captain King arranged but the escape attempt failed because the barque couldn't be found in the dark. Raleigh left the quay at Radford and travelled to the Cattewater and then returned undiscovered. A story refers to him hiding in Radford cave but this would seem unlikely. After five weeks at Radford, Raleigh was taken to London, an elderly man of 66 years and not in the best of health.

It is pleasant to consider that although under house arrest this famous Englishman who was a writer, scholar, soldier and explorer spent his last few weeks of freedom in Radford. Sir Walter Raleigh was beheaded in New Palace Yard, Westminster, in October, 1618.

Fig. 11: Sir Walter Raleigh's home at East Budleigh (Hayes Barton), Devon. It is built in the normal E-shaped style of the period. Radford House would have been similar in appearance.

Fig. 9: Artist's impression of Sir Walter Raleigh and Sir Christopher Harris at Radford in 1618.

# CIVIL WAR

Radford passed to Sir Christopher's grandnephew John Harris, who represented Liskeard, Cornwall, in Parliament. During the Civil War (1642-1646) he garrisoned Radford in the Royalist interest and was granted the rank of Major General of Infantry. Plymouth declared for Parliament and endured a lengthy seige. Volume 6 of D. Lyson's *Magna Britannia* published 1822, records that: *Plymstock was the headquarters of the beseiging (Royalist) army, when Plymouth was invested by Colonel Digby, in September; and it continued to be one of the principal stations after Prince Maurice arrived with his army. The Royalists had batteries at Oreston and Mount Batten, in this parish, and a guard at Hooe.*

On 18th February, 1645, a rally of the Puritan garrison drove the Cavaliers from their quarters at Mount Stamford (a short distance from Radford), which Sir Richard Grenville's troops had attempted to hold. The Roundheads pushed their advance a considerable distance before turning their attention to an attack on Radford. It was probably at this time that the famous Harris banqueting silver, bearing London hallmarks dating from 1581, disappeared from Radford. Whether the silver had been destroyed or carefully hidden by a Roundhead looter remained a mystery until 16th December, 1827, when 23 of the original 31 pieces were miraculously discovered hidden beneath the ground on a farm near Brixton.

After a lengthy enquiry the silver plate was returned to a descendant of the original owner (John Harris of Radford) who sold it at auction on the 10th May, 1887, for £1,255.0s.16d. (Descendants of the Harris/Bulteel family still hold some items of this silver bearing the Harris coat of arms).

Fig. 8: Artists drawing of a likely armed conflict during the Civil War of the 1640s.

A contemporary re-enactment of a Civil War fight by the Order of the Sealed Knot.

# RADFORD HOUSE

An early illustration of Radford House can be found in a map (Fig. 20 on Page 7) dated 1643, which shows military emplacements during the Civil War. The map cannot be considered an accurate depiction of Radford House but it does give the impression that the cartographer differentiated between the various buildings depicted and would have given a fair impression of the house at that time. It is known that the original structure of the house consisted of a single block facing south to which two wings were subsequently added to form a U shape with a forecourt in the middle. As an Elizabethan structure it may well have formed a classic E shape (Fig. 11).

The house at this time would likely contain an enclosed courtyard on the north front with projecting upper storeys supported upon colonnades of timber pillars on the courts east and west sides. The earliest walls were built of "stone and cobb" and were in parts as much as 13 feet thick, as became apparent in 1922 during the course of plumbing works.

Apart from the various "parts" of Radford incorporated in the St. Keverne follys, the only other known item is the dining room fireplace currently located in the grounds of the new Radford House (located behind Barn Farm). William Paynes painting dated 1793 shows the house in its rebuilt state in the 18th century (Fig. 3). All other depictions are photographic and date from early this century.

Mr. G. W. Copeland of the Old Plymouth Society wrote at length about Radford House in the *Western Morning News* on Friday 3rd December, 1954. Most of the description he gave has been transferred to the plan of Radford (Fig. 21) which gives the location of his very descriptive observations of the house shortly before it was demolished.

Fig. 21: Plan of Radford House.

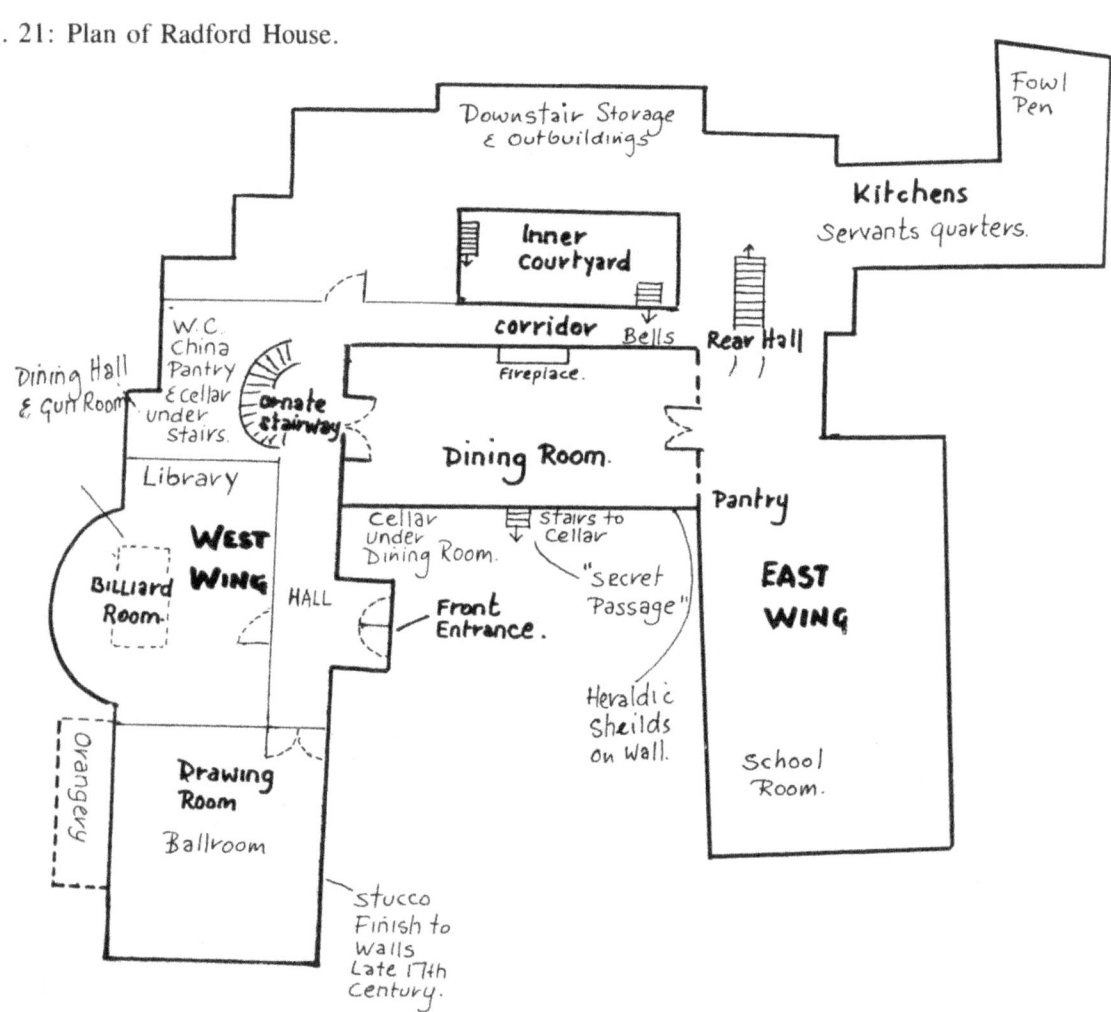

## DAPHNE DU MAURIER

Daphne Du Maurier, the novelist, included Radford in her adventurous tale *The King's General*. She described Radford House as ... *a great barracks of a place the other side of Plymouth*. The story, based on the Civil War, vividly portrays the flavour of the times. However, Miss du Maurier cannot recall ever seeing the house so the description can only be considered "author's licence".

Fig. 24:
Two close views of Radford House probably dating from the 1920s. The fine orangery is seen from two angles, the two large beech trees obscure part of the West wing which contained the billiard room, library and drawing room. Part of the parkland is included in the lower view with an ornamental fountain in the foreground.

Fig. 22:

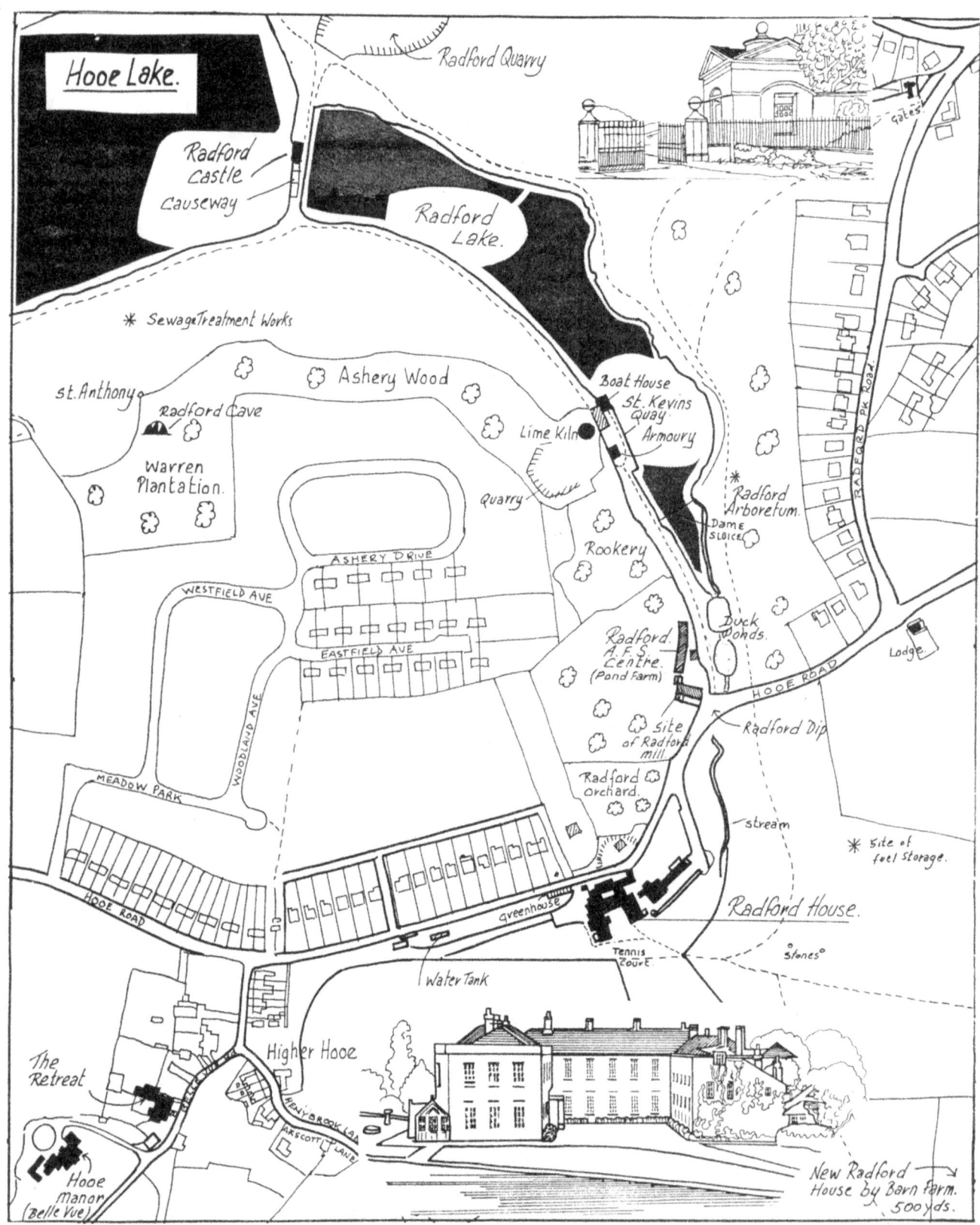

**The Radford Area**

This plan of the locality clearly shows the positions of the old and new houses and buildings occupying what was once Radford estate lands. The line drawings show the house (demolished 1935-7) and Radford Lodge which fortunately still stands although modified. A close look at this plan shows other buildings and the now familiar layout of modern roads and many houses. The lake forms the centrepiece of the area with the new Radford centre nearby.

Fig. 23: Various Views of Radford House and Grounds

The house and part of the extensive gardens taken around 1930.

Looking northwards towards the large mansion in the early 1930s. Modern houses and roads now cover much of this scene.

Part of the once well kept ornamental lakes and woods now known as Radford lake.

## HARRIS AND BULTEEL MARRIAGE

During the 17th and 18th centuries the Harrises lived on at Radford and progressively extended and modernised the mansion. Most of the original Elizabethan features were replaced or covered over with Georgian facades.

Many sash windows were installed. This was a period of growth for the Harris family and they spent much time in developing the whole estate — employing many local people in a variety of skills and trades. Descendants of these estate people still live in the locality.

In 1783 one of the Harris family married Catherine Bulteel, the daughter of John Bulteel of Flete. This instigated the convergance of the two families. During the next century members of the Harris/Bulteel family were occupying Radford itself and a number of houses adjoining the estate. These included *The Retreat*, circa 1760, and *Hooe Manor*, circa 1777, also known as *Belle Vue*.

As the century progressed the family prospered from their extensive banking interests. The Royal Naval Bank was established in 1774 and became the oldest bank in Plymouth. However, in 1914, the bank collapsed in disastrous circumstances. The two partners, Matthew Parker and Captain Bulteel, were put on trial at the Old Bailey which resulted in imprisonment for both men.

## RADFORD ESTATE SALE IN 1917

As a consequence of this event the entire estate (602 acres), was put up for auction. Following this devasting event, the solicitor acting as trustee of the estate in bankruptcy (Percy T. Pearce) placed the entire 602 acre estate up for sale by auction. The sale was conducted by Messrs. Andrew and Son at the *Royal Hotel* (blitzed in 1941), Plymouth, on Thursday 28th June, 1917. The auctioneers sale booklet, (Fig. 14) a copy of which is held in the local history section of Plymouth's Central Library, provides a wealth of details about the estate as it was in 1917.

The mansion, parklands, most of the farms, lodges and cottages were purchased outright by a respected local figure, William A. Mitchell (1861-1930) of nearby Rockville House, Pomphlett.

Hooe Manor was acquired by the flambouyant Colonel Coates and the *Retreat* by Mr. Arthur Spender (Mayor of Plymouth 1908-1909), whose children were all tragically drowned in Whitsands Bay.

### RADFORD ESTATE SALE.

#### £27,425 REALIZED.

Messrs. Andrew and Son, instructed by Mr. Percy T. Pearce, trustee in the Naval Bank bankruptcy, yesterday sold by auction at the Royal Hotel, Plymouth, the Radford estate. The estate, comprising residential and agricultural properties, was offered in forty lots. Competition for most of the properties was brisk, and all but a few changed hands. The total sum realized was £27,425, which was considered a very satisfactory figure.

The most valuable of the lots was Radford, the well-known family residence, with its pleasure grounds, gardens, magnificent woodlands, and dairy farm, occupying 263 acres, together with Barn Farm, containing 84 acres of pasture and arable land, six acres of rough pasture and woodlands and plantations covering 71 acres. Aggregate rental £772. The auctioneer estimated that in Radford Woods alone there were 3,000 trees worth not less than 30s. each. The bidding started at £3,000, and at £11,000 the hammer fell to Mr. William A. Mitchell, Rockville, Plymstock.

Hooe Manor, the second in importance of the lots offered, provoked no competition, and was withdrawn. It includes the attractive residence of "Hooe Manor" or "Belle Vue," an old-fashioned dwelling-house known as Holly Bank, and various enclosures of cultivable land and woodland, yielding an aggregate annual rental of £236.

The freehold farm, "Lower Goosewell," 147 acres, together with two enclosures of arable land, 11 acres, and an enclosure of woodland, yielding a total rent of £268, was bought by the tenant, Mr. William H. Jenkins, for £4,575.

"Higher Goosewell Farm," 75 acres, and let for £248, was purchased at £4,450 by Mr. Pedrick.

Goosewell-cottages. 16 in number, were sold singly for sums ranging from £130 to £190, and a total of £2,465. They are let at £10 each.

Other lots sold as follows:—Thorn Cot, Higher Hooe (rent £64), to Mr. James H. Ellis, Devonport, £850; Nos. 1 and 2, Arscott-lane, Higher Hooe, to Mr. Penwell, Wrangaton, £390; No. 3, Arscott-lane, £170, Mr. H. Hine; No. 4, Arscott-lane, £140, Mr. Potter; No. 5, Arscott-lane, £175, Mr. A. J. Page; No. 1, Radford-cottages, £235, Mr. F. J. Axworthy; No. 2, Radford-cottages, £180, Mr. Benmore; No. 3, Radford-cottages, £180, Mr. James H. Ellis; Nos. 4 and 5, Radford-cottages, withdrawn; 13 acres of accommodation land between Staddiscombe and Plymstock, £460, to Mr. R. B. Rapson, tenant; "Little Butts" building site, near Plymstock village, Mr. James, £290; No. 1, Furzehatt-villas, Plymstock (rent £45), £615, Mr. Down; No. 2, Furzehatt-villas (rent £28). £415, Mr. Whittaker; Bysland, accommodation and building land, 4 acres, £305, Mr. Potter; Higher Gopes and Simeon's Gopes, 11 acres of accommodation land, £500, Mr. J. C. Revell.

Five pieces of land, originally part of the Buenos Ayres building estate, were withdrawn.

Fig. 13:

The former pigs troughs can be seen embedded in the old lime kiln close to Radford lake presumably to make it look ornamental and in keeping with the lower buildings when they were complete.

Fig. 14:

In Bankruptcy.—No. 25 of 1914.   Re HARRIS, BULTEEL & Co., Naval Bank, Plymouth.

BY ORDER OF THE TRUSTEE.

# SOUTH DEVON,

Situate in a charming position within easy access and close to the important Naval Port and Military Centre of PLYMOUTH.

## PARTICULARS WITH PLANS & CONDITIONS OF SALE

OF THE HIGHLY IMPORTANT

## Freehold Residential and Agricultural PROPERTIES

KNOWN AS

# THE RADFORD ESTATE,

In the Parish of PLYMSTOCK, and comprising

## The Mansion House known as "Radford,"

Conveniently placed in Well Timbered Park-like Lawns with Charming Pleasure Grounds and Terraced Walks, Ornamental Ponds, Miniature Lake, Entrance Lodge, and Well Timbered Woodlands with Excellent Sporting attractions; another

**Charming Residence** known as 'Hooe Manor,' otherwise 'Belle Vue,'

Occupying a commanding position with Well-arranged Pleasure Grounds, Walks and Paddock;

ALSO A

**DETACHED FREEHOLD RESIDENCE** with Gardens and Stabling accommodation, known as "THORN COT," Higher Hooe.

**Two Well-built Semi-Detached VILLAS known as 1 & 2 Furzehatt Villas,**
PLYMSTOCK.

## Capital Farms with Residences and Homesteads

known as "Higher Goosewell," "Lower Goosewell," "Barn Farm," and "Radford Farm," Accommodation Pasture Lands, numerous Private Dwellings, Cottages and Gardens, Orchards and Tea Gardens.

## ATTRACTIVE BUILDING SITES

Comprising the whole of the unsold portions of "The Buenos Ayres Building Estate," admirably adapted for the erection of Villa Residences,

## The whole extending to an Area of about 602 Acres,

AND

## Producing a Rental of about £2,072 per annum,

WHICH WILL BE OFFERED FOR SALE BY AUCTION, BY

# MESSRS. ANDREW AND SON

At the "ROYAL HOTEL," Plymouth, on THURSDAY, the 28th day of JUNE, 1917, at Two o'clock in the Afternoon, in suitable lots.

*To View the respective Properties application should be made to the Auctioneers.*

Particulars with Plans and Conditions of Sale may be obtained of the Auctioneers, 10, Princess Square, Plymouth; or of

Mr. PERCY T. PEARCE,

*(The Trustee of the Estate in Bankruptcy),*

SOLICITOR, 10, PRINCESS SQUARE, PLYMOUTH.

LOT 11—continued.

# THE WELL-KNOWN FAMILY RESIDENCE

**OCCUPYING A SHELTERED POSITION,**

*Approached by a Wide Carriage Drive through Beautifully Timbered Lawns,*

## Is a Commodious Structure and Substantially Erected,

Combining dignity and unity of appearance, and the Internal Accommodation affords the necessary requirements of a Country Residence for the occupation of a family of position.

☞ The Mansion was renovated under the supervision of a celebrated Architect, the enriched panelling, cornices, architraves, carved pediments and other decorative work, bearing testimony of exquisite taste and beautiful design.

## The Accommodation of the Mansion

IS AS FOLLOWS:

**ENTRANCE PORCH and LOFTY ENTRANCE HALL and CORRIDOR
in which there is an Iron Deed or Plate Closet.**

The DRAWING ROOM.—A well proportioned apartment, 28 ft. 6 in. x 22 ft. 6 in., beautifully decorated and fitted with mahogany doors.

The BILLIARD ROOM—of fine proportions, with Bow Windows, overlooking the Pleasure Grounds on the Western side, 28 ft. x 22 ft., fitted with mahogany doors, and communicating with the Drawing Room.

The LIBRARY—adjoining the last mentioned, 23 ft. 6 in. x 15 ft. 6 in., with mahogany doors.

The DINING HALL—of noble proportions, 30 ft. x 18 ft., with windows facing South, with oak panelled walls with dado and cornice, 8 ft. 6 in. high, and carved overmantel.

The GUN ROOM—communicating with the last mentioned apartment.

Lavatory, China Pantry and Cellar under Staircase.

### THE MAIN STAIRCASE

*with Carved Oak Handrail and Panelled Oak Dado ascends in easy flights to the*

**FIRST FLOOR**—upon which is:

The Lofty Corridor leading to the principal Bed Chambers in the West Wing, consisting of:—

A Well-proportioned Bedroom with Dressing Room communicating.

A Spacious Bedroom, 27 ft. 6 in. x 22 ft., with bow front, and Dressing Room communicating.

Another Bedroom, 17 ft. 6 in. x 13 ft. 6 in., and Dressing Room communicating.

On the **HALF LANDING**.—The Bath Room, and Lavatory Basin, w.c., with h. & c. supplies.

**Secondary Bathroom** with h. & c. supplies.

The Blue Bed Chamber, 18 ft. 6 in. x 18 ft. 6 in.

The Pink Bed Chamber               do                      and Dressing Room adjoining.

LOT 11—continued.

IN THE EAST WING:

The Spacious Schoolroom.  Night Nursery and Maid's Bedroom.
Three Servants Bedrooms.

There are also 4 Secondary Bedrooms, Bath Room and Five Attics.

## The Domestic Apartments

**are fully commensurate with the requirements of a good establishment, and include:**

Butler's Pantry, China Cupboards, Servants' Hall, Lamp Room, Spacious Kitchen, another Kitchen, Dairy, Larders, Scullery and other domestic Offices.

The Cellars run underneath a portion of the House.

**THE OUT-DOOR OFFICES in the Court Yard at the rear of the Residence,**

consist of: Coal House, Wood House and Game Larder and Fowls' House.

**On the West Side of the Residence is the CONSERVATORY, 28 ft. x 15 ft.,**

in excellent condition.

### THE SANITARY ARRANGEMENTS

*are believed to be eminently satisfactory and have been recently reconstructed with up-to-date requirements.*

---

**The House is well preserved internally and in excellent decorative repair.**

---

### ON EACH SIDE OF THE RESIDENCE WILL BE FOUND

## The Delightful Pleasure Grounds

which are of considerable extent and exquisitely disposed in TERRACES, LAWNS, and FLOWER GARDENS, traversed by Sheltered Gravelled Walks.

The MAIN TERRACE—supported by a Stone Wall, having a Broad Walk, and flanked with Stately Specimen Trees and Ornamental Flower Beds, is a distinct feature.

THE GROUNDS contain beautiful Specimens of Forest Timber, Luxuriant Shrubs and Evergreens,
**Commanding Delightful Home Scenery.**

## The Capital Walled Gardens are amply stocked with a variety of choice Fruit Trees

AND INCLUDE THE FOLLOWING:

### GLASS AND OTHER HOUSES:

FERNERY, 22 ft. long; Tool House and Potting Shed; PEACH HOUSE, 50 ft. long; TWO VINERIES, 52 ft. long, with the necessary heating apparatus, Boiler House, Garden Frames and Forcing Pits, Store & Apple Chamber.

**AT A SHORT DISTANCE FROM THE MANSION AND VERY CONVENIENTLY LOCATED IS**

## The Range of Stabling, Coach-House and Garage,

CONSISTING OF

A Stable for 3 Horses with Hay Passage and Loft over.
Harness Room.                Cleaning Room.                                2 Trap Houses.
Another Stable for 4 Horses. Coach House           and                     Motor Garage.

### A SPACIOUS BARN

in which is a SAW BENCH, CHAFF CUTTER, and CORN MILL, worked by an ENGINE, by E. S. Handley, with Vertical Boiler, and a large cement Water Tank for feeding the Engine; WOOD SHED covered with corrugated iron; CIDER CELLAR and CARPENTER'S SHOP over.

## WILLIAM A. MITCHELL

William Mitchell (Fig. 15) had first gained prominence rather unexpectedly at the early age of five when he had the misfortune to fall into the waters of Pomphlett Creek. The *Western Morning News* of September, 1866, reported that he was rescued by one Thomas Marshall who ... *grasped the little one, and, by the aid of a friendly rope was helped on shore with his burden, both child and his rescuer being much exhausted.*

By 1917 Mitchell had become the largest landowner in the area and his holdings encompassed much of Pomphlett, including the ancient tide grist corn mills (demolished 1968). He was very active in public life, serving on all tiers of local government, and was a notable benefactor to innumerable improvement schemes and charities. Preferring to continue residing in his Edwardian villa, he let out Radford House to various tenants. During the First World War soldiers were billeted there. Tenants included Colonel Parker, Mrs. Jerratt Bell and finally the estate lodge keepers, Mr. and Mrs. Hines. The latter regularly escorted conducted tours of the house embellishing their commentaries with colourful stories of haunted secret corridors and hidden treasures.

William Mitchell died of a sudden heart attack on the 5th February, 1930, whilst addressing the County Council at Exeter Castle, leaving a substantial proportion of his fortune to charities. Radford House and the residue of the estate passed in trust to his fifteen year old son W. A. Gordon Mitchell (1915-1968). However, the house itself was fast deteriorating through lack of use and rampant vandalism and many of its valuable furnishings and fittings had been damaged or stolen.

The trustees, Mrs. William Mitchell and Charles Everson, employed various experts to examine the building and to recommend possible schemes for the restoration of the whole or even part, but the structure was found to be so unsound that the cost of repairs would have been prohibitive. It was, therefore, inevitable that in 1935, despite vigorous local representations, the trustees came to the reluctant conclusion that there was no alternative but to demolish the house. The trustees' decision was put into effect in 1937 when a Plymstock contractor, Harold Triggs, and six men demolished the house so thoroughly that not a single fragment was to remain. However, the parkland, gardens, farms, lodges and cottages were retained and in the late 1940s, Gordon Mitchell, F.R.I.C.S., built a small modern house amid the woods on the estate's higher lands, overlooking Plymouth, which assumed the name *Radford House*. In the grounds of this house lies a substantial granite fireplace lintel, which came from the dining room of Radford House (Elizabethan).

In 1956 Gordon Mitchell transferred most of the north park, its eighteenth century domed lodge and fine entrance gates, together with Radford Lake and its adjoining outbuildings, to Plympton Rural District Council, now under Plymouth City Council, and this remains a pleasing and important recreational area today. The Mitchell's fifty-year tenure of the Radford estate ended during the 1960s when the remainder of the land was sold. Within a very short time the new owners were granted planning permission for a housing development.

Fortunately the development of the housing estate was restricted to the higher meadows of the valley and has, therefore, saved the park, lake and woods for us to enjoy.

Fig. 15:

William A. Mitchell (1861-1930) and his wife Priscilla Littleton Mitchell (1876-1946). He lived at Rockville House, owned Radford estate, Pomphlett Mill and other local properties. Bertrand Gale, chauffeur to W. A.

Fig. 16:
Bertrand Gale, chauffeur to W. A. and G. Mitchell seen here about 1930.

## RADFORD LODGE

The original structure of this gatehouse was built in about 1750. Its purpose was simply to provide accommodation for the gatekeeper to Radford House.

Set at the top of a hill overlooking Radford and Hooe Lakes it is not hard to imagine the grandeur of travelling by coach through the gates and down to the house.

This lodge is one of the few remaining indications of Radford's greatness. Still evident are the large octagonal gate piers with their ball finials. In 1986 the building was in ruins but due to the dexterity of the renovators it was reconstructed and now retains much of the original looks.

In 1945, Mr. G. W. Copeland described the lodge as *aptly likened to a sweet jar stopper* and so it is. On the wall of the lodge an inscription tells of its historical connections with Radford House. The plaque was lost in the 1950s but fortunately it was found and restored to its rightful place.

The photograph that is shown is of the lodge in the early part of the century with the lodgekeeper Mrs. Repath. Her husband, always immaculately dressed, would greet visitors to the lodge with a *doom and despair* quotation from the Bible! Other known residents were Miss Emily Charlick and her mother and a lady known as Granny Davies. The original gates to this lodge were understood to have been fitted to the old Grammar School at Plympton St. Maurice.

Fig. 12: Radford lodge.

## RADFORD CASTLE

The building was erected as a lodge at the time the present dam was constructed circa 1860. It was used as accommodation for the "Keeper" responsible for supervising the estate moorings and quay, as well as other caretaking duties. It is made from the limestone of Radford Quarry and the castle was also known locally as *Jack's Castle*.

There have been many gate keepers. The family names Blatchford, Edwards and Stephenson within living memory. The castle was referred to by W. G. Copeland as a pseudo gothic castellated gatehouse, which probably means it would be ideal for a Dracula movie. It was once occupied in the 1930s by a Mr. Edwards and his family.

It had no bathroom (just a tin bath) and water had to be gathered outside. The archway once housed two white gates which were opened by the Edwards family whenever the residents of Radford came that way. Also boat owners who required access to the quay had to come through these gates. The last known residents of Radford Castle was the Stephenson family. It has since been used as an artist's studio and now is being developed as a Craft Centre for Social Services.

Fig. 12a: The Castle.

# RADFORD CAVES

These were not acknowledged or documented before the beginning of the century although some references suggest that Sir Walter Raleigh hid in the caves during his abortive escape and this is the reason for the term Raleigh's cave being used in some papers.

However, this limestone cave was entered frequently by local boys who used candles. They explored the passages looking for Drake's lost gold and searched for the tunnel reputedly connecting with the Radford House. An article in the *Western Morning News and Daily Gazette* of 27th July 1935, carried the following story:

## HIDING PLACE MYSTERY
### Search by *Morning News* Representative

Unfortunate as this decision is, it will produce a thrilling sequel as the old house is taken down. The entrance to a tunnel through which the residents fled centuries ago from Puritan attackers will be revealed.

Yesterday a *Western Morning News* representative searched the house and district for traces of this secret hiding place.

Near Radford Lake he found one end of the tunnel. It is a rift in the ground through which a man must crawl on hands and knees to enter. Then, by way of various subterranean caves and passages, the tunnel, which up to this point has been natural, develops into a stone structure. Unfortunately the air then becomes too foul to permit further exploration.

Where does the tunnel end? Does it connect with the house, as legend asserts? There is probably a hidden doorway in the old mansion. It may be in a fireplace or beneath the floor. It may even join with one of the secret passages which are believed to lie behind the panels on the wall. There is fascinating speculation in the secrets of the tunnel, for it is fully half a mile long, and has never been traversed within living memory. Before the work of demolition was started all walls and floors were tapped in an endeavour to find the secret passage, but without success.

Mr. W. A. Gordon Mitchell, the last owner of the cave, was familiar with the chambers and appeared in two newspaper publications that featured the cave. He also was responsible for locking the entrance to avoid accidents happening.

The cave is now controlled by The Plymouth Caving Group and the secret tunnel has still not been found.

Fig. 17: W. A. Gordon Mitchell (1915-68) with his eldest son, Nigel Gordon Mitchell emerging from Hooe Cave in 1952.

# GHOSTS AND MYTHS OF RADFORD

There are several ghosts associated with Radford which considering its age is not so surprising.

Take the ghost of a monk in full habit who was seen on many occasions to be at the lodge gates but no one ever saw his face! Servants at the house heard the industrious sound of *something* chopping wood and drawing water beneath their windows and they were convinced it was the monk (who appeared to be very restless).

There is also the account of a strange animal with saucer eyes which scared the servants. The occupier at that time, Major Anstis, forebade servants to take anything, (even food), from the house because this apparently aggravated the animal apparition.

Towards the end of its days the house seemed to protest at being abandoned because when it was unoccupied, in the mid 1930s, bells, long disconnected in the servants quarters, could be heard ringing at night and dogs whimpered on passing by.

However, there is no doubt that the most popular ghost is that of the *White Lady of Radford*. No one seems to know her origin but word has it that she was one of several girls living at Radford in the 18th century. It is said that she made friends with a local boy from nearby Oreston, but her parents forbade her to see him because of his lowly rank. However, she left the house (with the help of a maid servant) intent on disregarding her parent's wishes. As was her habit, she always wore white in the summer and so it was on this particular day when she met the young man. They took the boat across the lake which capsized drowning both of them.

Some say she has been seen sitting beside the lake and others have seen her in the grounds looking for her lost love. Many sightings have been made; a railwayman cycling home through Radford dip in the early morning had seen her and a reporter from the local paper driving past also saw her.

In the heyday of this tale, servant girls at the house dressed a broom as *the White Lady*, placed it at the foot of the butlers bed who, when awakened, was convinced the White Lady Ghost had come to visit him.

Neill P. G. Mitchell (son of the last owner of Radford) recalls that Bertrand Gale, chauffeur to both his father and grandfather, used to take conducted tours through the deserted corridors of Radford prior to its demolition. He was a good storyteller and used to put the fear of God into his charges with tales of ghosts and Raleigh yarns and then, when all was hushed, he would drop a heavy hammer causing much panic!

Fig. 18: The White Lady?                Fig. 19: The Faceless Monk?

## ST. KEVERNE'S QUAY (ST. KEVINS)

In this spot the ruins of two buildings stand both dating circa 1850. They were occupied by estate staff prior to their deterioration. The boathouse and the armoury were constructed to enhance the appearance of the area and also to provide adequate accommodation for the estate workers. Both buildings incorporate some genuine pieces from the old house of Radford. The boathouse contains the facade of a 16th century house with well moulded doorway heads and two granite pillars flanking the entrance door. The armoury has a granite front doorway reputed to be the original front door of Radford although this seems too small for such an important House. It would be nice to know for sure. A fireplace within the armoury is made of granite and carries a fleur-de-lys motif and the date 1640 — certainly coming from Radford House (Fig. 6, Page 6).

A further ruin stands close by to St. Kevernes which is a limekiln built to look like a castle. It also contains some granite pig troughs and parts of a cheese or apple press forms the door lintel (Fig. 13, Page 14). Another press lies in the ground by the boathouse. There can be little doubt that this spot was the quay to Radford before the houses were built. It is well recorded that many dignitaries visited Radford including Drake and they would all have landed here with quick access to the mansion.

In the woods above the quay a quarried area exists which once contained a terraced walk and wooden summer house (Fig. 24).

Fig. 25: St. Kevern's Quay between 1884-1900 showing display gardens and the summer house in the woods.

## THOMAS RADFORD

On 3rd April, 1774, John Harris of Radford the then owner of the estate and a senior partner in the Naval Bank in Plymouth, registered for baptism a Thomas Radford. Not too remarkable until a glance at the parish records revealed that Thomas was a negro belonging to John Harris.

The idea of negro slaves conjures up visions of *Gone With The Wind* but in this case it was probably a strong Christian motivation from John Harris that actioned the baptism.

John Harris died only four years later and the estate passed to his nephew, another John Harris. Of Thomas Radford the only other information is that he was buried in 1793.

The only other reference to the name of Radford after this time was in a bequest of £100 to *John Radford of the Naval Bank* from another John Harris (who was the great nephew of Thomas Radford's master). Although there is no evidence to suggest a relationship between the two Radfords, it would be nice to think so.

## THE MAN WHO WAS ROBINSON CRUSOE

In the early 18th century a resident of Oreston was Alexander Selkirk whose castaway experiences were immortalised in Daniel Defoe's famous novel, *Robinson Crusoe*. Selkirk married the widow Frances Candis (an Innkeeper in Oreston) and settled there for a while. However, he returned to the sea and eventually died on it in 1720. We know from his last will and testament, dated 12th December, 1720, that he was mate on the ship H.M.S. *Weymouth* in which he was about to sail. He did sail but died at sea.

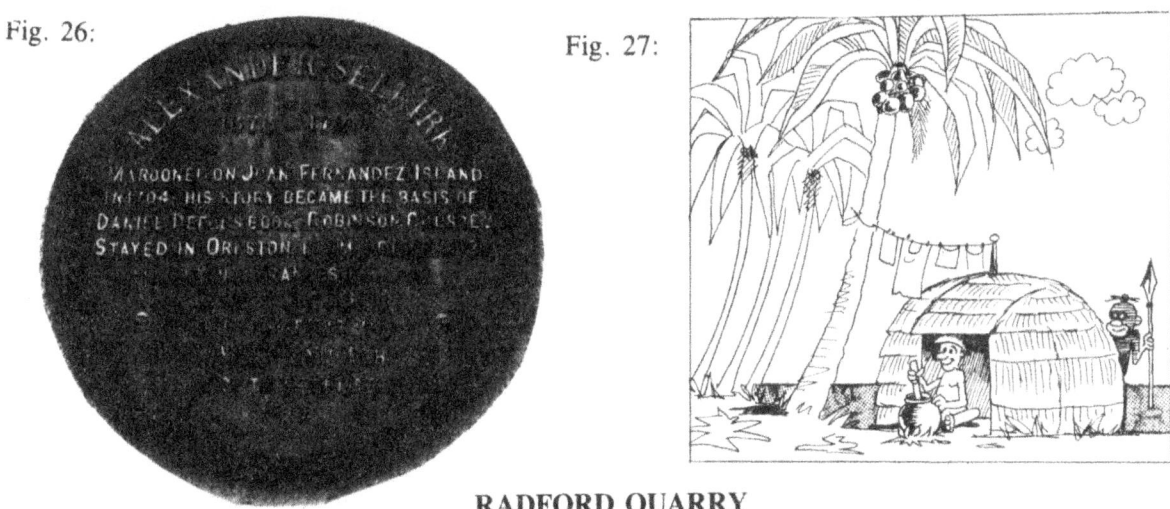

Fig. 26:

Fig. 27:

## RADFORD QUARRY

Radford Quarry was excavated early in the 1800s to meet part of the massive requirements of building the Plymouth Breakwater. The quarry was worked for more than 50 years and provided employment for many quarrymen as well as long term employment for the many boatmen transporting the stone across the Sound. Two quarries were used to supply the stone, Hooe and Radford. The Breakwater was completed in 1846.

## LAWRENCE OF ARABIA AND THE ROMAN ALTAR

During his short period at R.A.F. Mount Batten, T. S. Lawrence was often observed travelling through Radford Dip on his motorcycle. He had an active interest in Radford and it is thought that he subscribed to the theory that Radford had "Roman" origins, a rather controversial theory for a short while. This was based upon a short granite pier or shaft located within one of Radford's north eastern stables.

The appearance of this shaft, set against the concave limestone wall, was reminiscent of a shrine. Hence the name "Roman Altar". This stone, acccording to G. W. Copeland, is in the garden of a private house in Plymstock and an examination has shown it was probably a pedestal intended to support some type of sculpture.

The north east view of Radford House in the summer of 1930. The dormer window wing was the oldest part of the mansion's fabric.

The Retreat (above) and Hooe Manor also known as Bellevue were built for members of the Harris/Bulteel families and were once part of the Radford estate. They have been occupied by various well known families such as Colonel Thomas W. Hicks at Bellevue and Major William H. Hare at the Retreat.

# Arthur L. Clamp – the man behind the books

Arthur Leslie Clamp was a man of boundless energy with a passion for helping others, particularly through his love of history. A printer by trade, he started his career in a printing company before moving his family from Exeter to Plymouth to teach at the Plymouth College of Art and Design, where he eventually became the Head of the Printing Department.

## A Devoted Family Man

*Arthur with his five children.*

Despite his love of teaching, Arthur prioritised his family, always making it home by 5:30pm for tea. He and his wife, Rosemary, raised five children: Susan, Angela, Elizabeth, David, and Steven. Arthur would often combine his love of family and history by taking his children on Sunday walks, encouraging them to appreciate historical monuments by taking photos or making crayon rubbings of gravestones for his books. The family home at 203 Elburton Road was a hub of activity, with a large garden, featuring a two-storey fort and a makeshift swimming pool.

## A Lifelong Learner and Adventurer

Arthur's thirst for knowledge extended beyond history to a deep curiosity about the world. He was passionate about exploring different cultures, traditions, and cuisines, often taking advantage of his long summer holidays as a teacher to travel to places like India, Russia, South America, the middle east and the USA, sometimes bringing one of his children along. This adventurous spirit even influenced his home life, as seen by the short-lived family tradition of steam-cooking vegetables after a trip to Iceland.

*History is a prominent feature of family days out*

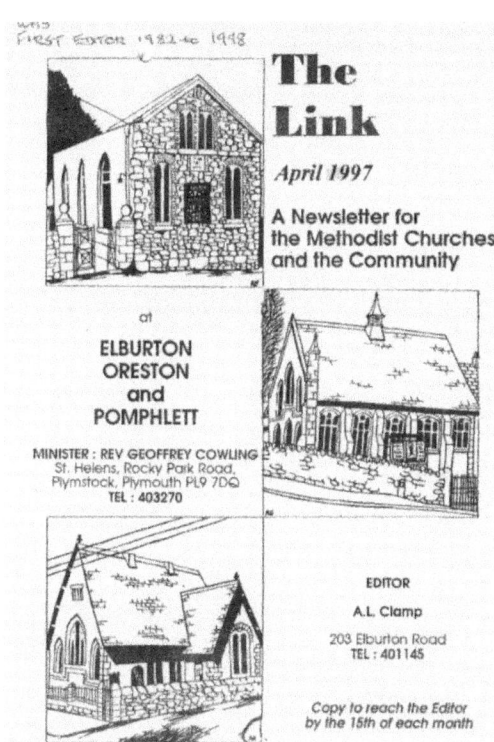

## Community and Philanthropic Spirit

His commitment to serving others was evident in his long-standing involvement with the Elburton Methodist Church. He was the Sunday School Superintendent for over 15 years and served as the editor of the wider church's monthly newsletter, "The Link," for a similar duration. After Rosemary's very sad passing, Arthur later remarried and, following a chance encounter with a professor from India, established a connection with a missionary school in Chennai. Together with his new wife, Christine, he co-founded a "Sponsor a Child's Education" program that continues to this day.

*Pictured left – The cover of 'The Link' complete with hand drawn sketches of each church by Angela*
*Below right – Arthur Clamp promoting his latest book*
*Below left – Arthur at home with his first wife, Rosemary*
*Below centre – Arthur on holiday with his second wife, Christine*

## A Legacy of Learning and Positivity

Arthur's greatest passion was history, which he brought to life through tireless research, documentation, and the many books he authored. He was driven by a need to "never be stuck in a rut," constantly seeking new experiences, meeting new people, and expanding his knowledge. With a positive attitude and a great sense of humour, he was always ready to help others, leaving a lasting impact on his family and community. His children, Susan, Angela, Elizabeth, David, and Steven, remember him with love and gratitude.

David Clamp, 2025

## A Legacy of Local History

Below is the story of how Arthur L Clamp began writing books, in his own words, drafted shortly before he passed away in 2001. I have only made minor alterations to this text, correcting grammatical errors that he did not survive to correct himself. When I first discovered this text, I was shocked to see my name mentioned. It seems that, unbeknownst to me, I shared my first PC with him. I suspect he used it during the day when I was at school, although I do have one memory of sitting with him and showing him how it worked. It has been a pleasure to pick up where he left off and see his books republished and redistributed, and to know that I was part of the story, even back then. It was also fascinating to discover that his pricing structure matches the way I have tried to price the books, with a third going to local sellers and the rest covering printing costs with a little left over for my expenses.

I am his eldest grandson, and it is a privilege to curate his legacy, which we are calling 'The Clamp Collection'. The very last line of the text originally reads "The following pages list all the titles." Sadly, that page is missing and we have no record of all the books he published and knowing that some of those were researched by other authors makes the process of finding them even harder. I look forward to one day completing the collection and seeing them all available again. And maybe, one day, I'll even start writing my own to add to the series. For now, here is his story in his own words.

Steven Gibson, 2025

## Writing and Publishing Booklets on Local Topics and Areas

I started this interest in either 1968 or 1969 when living in Woodford. I had by these dates established the Department of Printing and I think I must have been looking for something different to do. The first titles were of A5 size proofed from type set at Clarke, Doble and Brendon, Ltd., Plymouth printers, and then made up into pages and printed at Sawtell and Neilson, Ltd., Totnes.

Then began a slow process of getting them out to shops, etc. which proved to be more time consuming and difficult than actually researching, writing and getting the books into print. However, I persisted and opened a business account with Barclays Bank on the Broadway. I was advised to give it a title so I called it "Westway Publications". There came along another problem, one of storage of paper and finished books which was solved when the family moved to Elburton in 1970.

I changed the printer to Penwell, Ltd., Callington, Cornwall, as he was then just setting up himself and his prices seemed very reasonable. I did not get any of the printers to make up the complete books. I hand folded the flat printed sheets, stitched the books on a small manual table stitcher and trimmed them in a small hand turned guillotine which I bought from someone in Penzance for £40. It was brought up in a van.

The trouble and time going to and fro to Callington was too much so I transferred the printing to PDS Printers, Prince Rock, Plymouth, and I have been with them ever since. Now they are at Plympton which is easy to reach and they fold the flat sheets which was turning out to be a long chore which only saved a small part of the printing costs.

All my first titles were written by myself. I took the photographs and developed them in the loft of the house, the type was set by now on a computer situated in the house at Elburton from which I had collected photographic lengths of text to cut up and law down as pages.

At some point I decided that I would do my own film processing of lith film so I bought a large second hand process camera from Kingsbridge and learnt through trial and error to make line negatives of the text and halftone negatives of the illustrations which proved more difficult than I anticipated. The main problem was trying to keep the developer in the large dish at the correct temperature as any change would affect the developing time. I replaced this old camera with a brand new one bought from Croydon, Surrey, costing £900. This has turned out to be a great asset cutting out an expensive part of the printer's costs and one crucial aspect of the work which I could control.

By the middle 1970s there were many outlets I had contacted in Plymouth, up to Dartmoor, Exeter, around to Torbay, Totnes, Dartmouth and the South Hams. The market for local books was much greater than I had first thought and through getting to know many local people undertaking research themselves had the chance to help and make up books for other people who had in most instances, got together a collection of photographs with some text in a rather muddled way. Through my experience in print I was able to shape up their work and get it into print and in every case I had to pay the printer and let the person have the royalties. In the majority of titles produced in this manner this was another way of producing titles and it did give some profit to my work. However, I must say that in a few cases I lost out by either the other person getting the numbers wrong, not returning any monies from stock I delivered or they thought that more of their books should have been sold.

The print run was usually 1,000 copies and from time to time I have had reprints of 250 copies. It took about ten years to clear the first print run so I always had large stocks in the garage, workshop, etc. The numbers sold during the early years was about 7,000 copies a year increasing to around 9,000 copies and for the whole of the enterprise about 500,000 have been sold. The booklets have become part of the local scene and many people collect them, shops regularly order copies and I go around certain areas month by month restocking or replacing titles as necessary.

During the past year or so I have started setting the text on a Packard Bell PC, something which I should have done some years back. I share it with Steven Gibson, my grandson. There appears to be no end to the market for local books, but I could not earn a regular income because of the long time it takes to sell stock.

However, now exceeding 100 titles made up mainly of A4 twenty-four page booklets, some folded guides, with selling prices set with a third going to the shop which is the trade custom, the original idea has been quite successful and could go on for ever.

Apart from monetary benefits, however spasmodically these might be, I have learnt a lot myself, met many interesting people and have become part of the local scene with requests to give talks and to advise people about getting into print.

Arthur L Clamp, 2001

Friday, August 17, 2001 (PPI)

# Death of local historical author

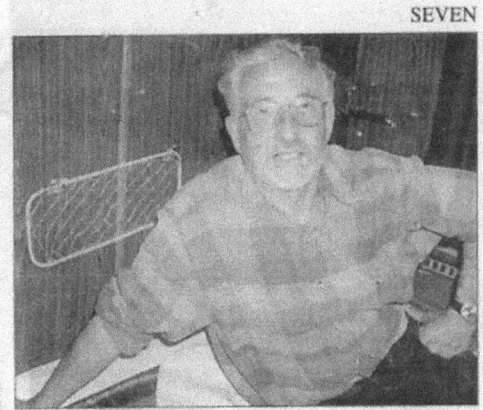

'He was an incredible character who was just loved by everybody who knew him'

A WELL-loved Elburton author has died at the age of 68.

Arthur Clamp (pictured right), who was one of the West Country's most successful writers, died at St Luke's Hospice, Turnchapel, after losing his battle against cancer.

Tributes have been flooding in for a man who was known in the community as a prominent writer and outgoing person.

He produced more than 140 titles during his life, dealing with both fiction, fact and history, often discussing West Country topics that were close to his heart.

One of his most acclaimed books was *The Plymouth Blitz*, and he also won credit for *The Rise and Fall of the Bearings of Membland Hall*, set in Noss Mayo.

He achieved sales of between 7,000 and 9,000 books every year and it is estimated that he has sold over half a million books, covering the areas of Plymouth, Dartmoor, Exeter, Torbay and the South Hams.

Mr Clamp was born in Mitcham, Surrey, in 1932, and was the eldest of four children.

He moved to Devon in 1941 to avoid the London air-raids.

Mr Clamp trained as a printer in Exeter and also gained a teachers' certificate in 1959 from Garnet College in London.

Plymouth College of Art, however, was to prove to be Mr Clamp's working home for the following 32 years until 1991, when he retired as head of the printing department.

He had a great interest in travel and had visited the USA, Tanzania, China, Russia, Peru, as well as travelling across Europe, where he presented talks and slide shows on his experiences as a writer.

Mr Clamp was a member of Elburton Methodist Church for many years, superintendent of the Sunday school and editor of the church newsletter, as well as being involved in much charity work.

He was president of the Plymouth and District Field Club and an active member of the Elburton Residents' Association.

He enjoyed leading walks on Dartmoor and historical tours throughout the West Country.

Mr Clamp married his first wife, Rosemary, in 1956 and they had five children – Susan, Angela, Elizabeth, David and Steven – and she died in 1987. He also had 11 grandchildren.

He leaves a wife Christine, after remarrying in 1991, and her two children and three grandchildren.

'He was an incredible character who was just loved by everybody who knew him,' said his wife.

'He will be missed by his family, his friends, the people he worked with and just everybody who knew him through his books.'

More than 300 mourners attended his funeral at Elburton Methodist Church on Monday.

The attendance was a celebration of his life – he would have found that really special. It shows his vibrancy and love of people,' said Mrs Clamp.

Steven Clamp added that his father was 'a well respected and loved man, missed by a great many people throughout the South West and far beyond'.

This newspaper article, published by the Evening Herald on 17th August 2001, forms a good record of his life. Just as he encourages us to learn more about local history, we encourage you to learn a little about him. For that reason, we have included these pages at the back of all the most recently republished books, in honour of his memory and recognition of his contribution to the community.